This book was written by

_____

_____

_____

I love it when you

_____

_____

_____

You are good at

_____

_____

_____

You inspire me to do many things, especially

_____

_____

_____

I always smile when you

I love doing many things with
you especially

_____

_____

_____

I love
when you teach me to

_____

_____

_____

And
when you tell me not to

_____

_____

_____

My fondest memory of us is when

_____

_____

_____

You cook me
delicious meals especially

You are special
because

_____

_____

_____

I
admire you because

_____

_____

_____

You always tell the story of the time when

_____

_____

_____

I'm thankful to you because

_____

_____

_____

You make me laugh when

_____

_____

_____

You should be
always

_____

_____

_____

You are
the kind of person that

_____

_____

_____

The most important thing you can do is

_____

_____

_____

My favorite memory with you is

_____

_____

_____

I appreciate
you most when you

_____

_____

_____

I love it when
we

_____

_____

_____

The funniest thing you do is

_____

_____

_____

My favorite thing
about you is

_____

_____

_____

I remember the time when you and me

_____

_____

_____

I am proud of you because

_____

_____

_____

I love you because

The best thing about you is

_____

_____

_____

My earliest memory
of you is

The most important lesson you ever taught me

_____

_____

_____

You are my superhero

You are awesome because

_____

_____

_____

You are my inspiration because

_____

_____

_____

You are my best friend because

_____

_____

_____

You are such a good

_____

_____

_____

I'll always remember the thing you have taught me

You are very
powerful you can do everything

You love it when I

_____

_____

_____

Our favorite thing to do together is

You taught me how to

You are the best

_____

_____

in the world

Thank you
for everything

Made in the USA
Monee, IL
21 April 2022